The Village and Other Poems

Poetry by Iain Crichton Smith from Carcanet

Selected Poems
A Life
The Exiles

IAIN CRICHTON SMITH

THE VILLAGE AND OTHER POEMS

CARCANET

Acknowledgements are due to the editors of the following magazines, newspapers and anthologies, where some of these poems first appeared: *Poetry Review, Poetry Book Society Anthology, Stand, PN Review, Scotsman, Listener, Spectator* and *Verse*.

First published in 1989 by
Carcanet Press Limited
208-212 Corn Exchange Buildings
Manchester M4 3BQ UK

British Library Cataloguing in Publication Data

Smith, Iain Crichton, *1928-*
    The village and other poems
    I. Title
    821'.914

    ISBN 0-85635-834-7

The Publisher acknowledges financial assistance from
the Arts Council of Great Britain.

Typeset in 10pt Palatino by Bryan Williamson, Manchester
Printed in England by SRP Ltd., Exeter

Contents

The Village

1.

My house of music,
I have left you behind
    for this garden
    blossoming in the country,
this sky
    plain and guiltless.
The busyness of feet,
    the drama of projects,
the distant city smile,
    all have been left behind
for this open ploughland.
    Here no shadows
slant from lamp-posts,
    the long black rays
of city clocks.
    And the beggar
does not doze
    under his newspaper:
and the chipmaker
    dressed like a stoker
    does not shovel chips
    out of his container.
Here, the bay
    is not a hive of yachts,
    wasp-striped, stingless:
and the wind-filled skirts
    do not breed tales.
My house of music,
    I shall not forget
    the debt I owe you,
    the flash of windows,
    the thresh of shadows,
the tree-lined avenues
    that never have an end.

2.

Graves invent nothing
in a country cemetery,
    aged and mossy:
and the stone bibles
    shine with ancestry
under the flicker of birds.
The minister winds his robes
    decently about him
as he shakes hands
    with all the live people
who at Easter time
    wear their flowery hats
in unchiming envy.
    Overhead, the clouds
    head for distant countries
in their changing marble:
    and the wheel of crocuses
returns each year
    above the mouldering chests.

3.

Gemeinschaft –
Katag at the bookstall
exchanging weather.
Everyone naming each other
in this calm air
    through which the water
glides, reflecting trees:
the weasels however anonymous
and the hares
    at whose throats they suck.

Smoke
    rises from bonfires
of bracken. Ash
badges the rowan tree.

4.

While the birds sweetly twitter
    I visit the old lady
    who reads Ouspensky
    and whose blue radio
converses among the glitter
    of random sunlight.
"I am frightened," she says,
    "of what I do not know."
    Is it of Death
with his negligent scythe
    familiar as Hugh
    under a blue sky?
"I do not know," she says.
    Just, "I am frightened."
    Her horned cows stare
    out of her meadow,
and the rabbits race through dew
    towards the weasel.

5.

At night
    I put out the ashes,
        and stand amazed
    beneath the blaze
        of a million million stars.

6.

The fox sings
    his song of slyness,
and lopes easily
    by the hedge:
and the spare hawk anchors
    by a cloud.
    By rabbit-watch
I walk clothed among the naked.
    Not by lamplight
does the harsh buzzard read his book,

nor change from black
will the ragged crow
whose language does not frame the No
of the soul's delicacy.

7.

Each morning
I cross the railway line

towards the kiosk
to collect my newspaper.

Summer,
how lovely you are,
how leafy,
just like a newspaper
composed of coloured paper.

And also the rails hum
towards the future
in the midst of such news returning,

those reds and greens.

8.

She walks,
mumbling to herself
    down this street,
big-bellied, round-faced.
She has found no one
    other than herself
    to talk to,
and her discussions
    are infinite.
Beyond her
the sea keeps its own music
    obsessive, self-absorbed,
    omnivorous.

Her lips move
    soundlessly,
    endlessly,
in that continuous gossip
    that never surprises.

9.

She has filled
    her life's emptiness with furniture.
"That chair is too good to sit on,
    and the carpet
    cost me five hundred pounds."
There is a vase
    of paper flowers on the television:
her suite
    is made of rich red velvet.
"Look at the view," she says.
    The sea, the sea,
stretches emptily to the horizon.
Envy is too simple a judgment
    for one who sits in her kingdom
    like a queen
whose servants have left her.
    It is autumn.
    She sees us to the door.
    I remember
the coffee had no real taste
    and for her talk
it was so full of chairs
    I stumbled over it.
Where there is emptiness
it has to be filled somehow.
This autumn fills it with leaves,
    which storm about her legs.

The little red van
buzzes about the village.

Letters from England, Canada, New Zealand.

We communicate with each other
        because of a driver
        with a small black moustache.

Little red van
        at the edge of the ocean
dodging among the trees
        with no salt on it.

The nest
        with one green egg in it
is suspended among the trees.
        The thrush has deserted it.

It is a tiny earth among straw,
cold now, without the throb of life in it.
Who has touched it with his hands
        and left the smell of man on it?

For the bird flies away
        and will not return.
I imagine how its wings mourn
        an absent greenness.

I should have loved Paris
        when Picasso was there
        or Braque,
when they stuck morsels of news
        to their paintings:
        when the concierge

was a cube
  like a French mountain:
and in gaunt attics
  the easels
thirsted for the paint.
  Excitement,
  discovery,
  a new world,
quotations from Africa,
  triangular faces like deer.

But I have to live
  where the black bibles
  are walls of granite,
where the heads are bowed
  over eternal fire.

13.

Last night
you attended a lecture on Vermeer
on the Island of Mull.

How clear
the mountains are,
and these rooms in which symmetry was humanised!

The deer
are elegant,
though the men have been prised
loose from their moorings.
In these pictures
such light, such light!
Remember the girl with the jar
pouring milk into the ewer,
her arms so muscular!
Or at a table the soldier
talking to his sweetheart.
Dutch maps on the walls.
The echoing bibles and the sails, the sails!
Under the green hills,

the exiled bodies.
Open the windows!
Let the light flood through!
Space, such endless space,
so framed by joy.

14.

The old lady is dying
among the roses,
    and at night
she hears the hoot of the owl,
the fluting of the blackbird,
the excited cry of the thrush.
    Doctor,
she knows well what is wrong,
she is adjusting her shoulders
to the stone cloak.
    She has put out the ashes
for the last time.
    And yet, who is dying
in this summer of stunning splendour
when the rhododendrons are ablaze
by the hedge,
    when the pansies
are bowed in thought,
    and the azaleas
are a constant fire?
    We are part of the earth,
its blackness nestles about us,
    and the rowan
is a constellation of blood drops.
    There is no sorrow
in the song of the blackbird,
    and the rabbit
runs easily towards its death.
    I have seen a cat
stiffly dead on the road,
    the crow pecking at it,
its eyes staring upwards
    in an illusion of agate:

and I have seen the children
    in their butterfly frocks.
    Summer, we love you,
there is no end to your manifestations,
to the freshness of your plots.
    The white curtain
in the bedroom of the old lady
freshens the window.
    A man is ploughing the land
with a red tractor.

15.

Today
    as the trees sparkle
    in the sunshine,
I remember my university days,
    the historian
who lectured on the French Revolution
    with exact primness.

Robespierre died in Aberdeen,
    and so did Danton,
    a whole structure
    of chandeliers fell.

And also
    Lear died on the moorland,
his crown melting
    in reality and age.

The trees sparkling,
    these tales I remember,
    and the clear
cemeteries also I recall
    on whose slabs I lay revising
Virgil's *Aeneid*.

16.

This morning,
the snow falling,
the children

are building a snowman.
How white it is.
How they toil

to shape it
behind the schoolhouse
with its chalky blackboards.

This blank squatness,
Buddha of silence,
beyond questions,

sitting in the world,
temporary art,
a structure of water.

17.

I read of *Sevastopol*
    by Tolstoy
    in a train going to my village.

This Russian is my contemporary,
    though my sky
    is Gaelic.

I hear the guns
    in the holy silence
    of your prose
    which casts its shadows,
Just as it was,
    bravery and cowardice.
    All the aristocrats
    whom I never knew
    in peasant Lewis
    dying like lilies
    which are unable to bend.

Writing
is easier than experience.
   In Halifax
you suffered the tax
   of exile,
and in dosshouses
     you nailed your shoes
     to the wooden floor.
     There is no sorrow
worse than the sorrow
     of the exile,
for he wakens early
     with ash in his mouth,
and there are only shadows
     in the world around him.
Open your purse
     to the shadowy exile:
     as for my book,
     leave it.
For pages do not starve,
     do not die of
the thirst of salt.
They can easily be remade,
     though not so the sails
     that reflect new sunsets.

Bags over shoulders
     the kids make their way
to the country school.
     There is a smell of roses
     and an untaught sky.

Geography is here
     in the wandering perfumes
and the chalk-white roads:
     where the larks sing high

above the scrawled bushes
and the dewy rowans
wear their red dresses
in these parishes of green.

20.

The raspberry tree
    arches the garden,
the crocuses
    are bent by the wind.

The small birds beat the rats
    to the bread,
among all that red
    and yellow and white.

Sun, you are shining
    from your old socket,
as Peggy carries her bags
    of groceries home.

How calmly the dead
    lie in their worn ground,
wrinkled like carbon
    above which the clouds call
    briefly, whitely.

21.

Death strides freely across the countryside,
    swinging his stick.
Sometimes he stops at a cottage
    where an old woman
is fraying fresh water
    from a bucket.
Sometimes he watches a weasel
    sucking the throat of a hare
    beside a rowan tree.
Sometimes he watches a cat
    trotting with a lark

through the shrubbery,
He takes out a cigarette and smokes it,
a small cloud at his mouth
and listens to a radio
playing Greensleeves.
Sometimes he knocks on a door
of a large house
where a man with white hair
is reading Everyman.
Death is a polite fellow
who loves azaleas
and the blur of bluebells.
'Without me they would not exist
without my sickle and scythe
without my empty circles.
And what would the shepherd be then
singing of his sweetheart?
And as for Greece or Rome,
beyond the Dark Ages
they shine like jewels of fire.'

22.

Days when the rain brims
the teeming barrels,
and plain wet windows
reflect no drama:
and the small birds peck
at the soaked bread.

Days when the clouds loom
over the chimneys,
and, like old women, the trees
forget themselves

in demented stories.

23.

It is a fine morning,
the frost is sparkling.
It is said of you, Raphael,
that you learned
    from Michelangelo,
from the study of armies.
    So happy you were,
contented creator,
    whose Virgin and Child
calmly foresaw their fate.
    It is a fine morning,
the frost is sparkling,
    glittering diamonds.
    Let me open my hands,
to the visitations of clouds.
    Let me see Florence
in these mountains of pure white.

24.

Hang out your washing
    like paintings
in the calm day.
    Raphael,
    Botticelli,
each beside the other
    in a gallery of blue.

Rag-darned goddesses,
    the sweat of the present
drying towards Venice
    and its fine cloudy towers.

Sundays, how awful they are.
    All day the grass does not change
    and the clouds that visit us
    drift off elsewhere.
    We try to think of
the beauties of religion but
    in fact we feel aggression,
    inward furies,
the torment of silence.
    Dear birds,
    flying from the south
can you bring us contentment?
    Can we hear in your tones
    the dry classical voices?
    Sundays,
when will the dead abandon us?
    When will the living
    no longer be a sacrifice
    to the gnaw in the bone?

The gates are open,
    let the stranger enter
    with dust on his feet
    all the way from Galilee,
    that serene profile.

26.

At Easter we sit in church.
    The organ pipes
are pointed like missiles.
    The minister
assails all nuclear arms (pushing
    a curl back from his brow).
What does he know of it, they think,
    the crofters, the wives.
    His passion
is, they would say, indecent
    among these calm gray graves
where their forefathers lie

    so placidly
having travelled their single rut
    on a bony cart
towards the cemetery.
    See,
the women's hats are like wheels,
    blue, green, purple,
    as the ball
sparkled high in the sky
above Japan,
    that "foreign"
unintelligible region.
    His plan
is, for the good, heaven,
    for the bad
an earth converted to ashes,
and the bushes
wearing their blossoms of grey.

27.

The cat
    brings the rabbit
    home between his teeth.

It is a gift
    to the lank god
    who feeds him,
to the magic
    that renews his dish.
    The rabbit mews
    piteously
more winning than the mouse
    with its tail of string.

    Stunned, it lies
under the cat's negligent gaze.
    To rescue it
    is, now,
    out of the question.
    That fatal blow

has brought it low
for this is a savage circuit
    on which the cat, lazily blinking,
    thornily turns.

28.

These roots stretch
    deeply into the soil
almost unpullable.
    White and tough,
    how can they know death,
    aged lady,
    who too die
    very slowly
so that you have to be tugged
    out of your chair
which is burning there
    in a priceless sunset.

29.

Today,
    you send me a letter
    from Lewis,
    saying
how much my writings mean to you,
    the tragedy, the comedy,
    the child who remembers
    and the man who grieves.

Island,
    you are moving away from me,
    and yet
    there is a mirror
    with images in it,
the headlands
    which wail of exiles,
    the stiles
over which ghosts leap
    like angels,

the daffodils
    that will yellow the moors,
    my remorse
for not being word perfect.

30.

    Altogether
you take 22 pills,
to keep you sound.
In your calm weather
you have little to do
    but, like water,
pass time in talk.
    Animals,
    we are talking animals,
    gregarious.
Without gossip
    we fade and die.

And sometimes more than gossip
    there is Homer,
    the very high stair,
    towards azure,
the former monkey can climb.

31.

    Our brains bulged
to differentiate us from the animals,
    and our eyes became bifocal.
    We could stand upright
and clutch the sharp stones.
    Fate
was on our side; to the local
we weren't tied, but could explore
by entering foreign doors.
    Tigers
we sank in pits,
    and we ate
    the marrow bones

24

of mammoths.
        O, the wind brought stories
to us, and in the fires too
        we saw the shadows of flesh,
and on the walls of caves
        we drew the first trembling strokes.
        Oaks
bowed to us.
        In the sunshine of April
we limped in rain. We prayed
to the clouds above.
        And then
galleries we made, draughty paintings.
        Food they became to us,
            poetry,
epics and tales on the breeze.

                    32.

Clumps of bees built
        their fences of sharp stings
        to protect their honey;
and the ants too
        learnt their grades and classes
on a fine morning.
        Hermit, you are strange
in your soiled blanket,
singing to yourself
under a slum of cloud.

                    33.

On a breezy morning
we visit the market.
The lady at the cosmetics stall
    is making up her face,
and another is trying on the opal
    of a new ring.
Clothes hang on rails
    above the dry people,
and the fiery curtains
    flutter bravely.

Pick up the toy horseman
who rocks backwards and forwards
    on his metal horse.

"How much in this world we don't have need of,"
    said bald Socrates,
strolling through the market
    on a Greek morning.

    I, on the contrary,
    love the sly
cries of the salesmen,
    who have to live, don't they,
    just like us
on this plenteous
    market most various
among white dishcloths and rings.

34.

Tonight the moon's so close
I could almost pull it towards me.
And I hear the dancers' feet
on the hall's bare boards.

The moon of autumn,
unrustable and red,
in which the sailor sees
his mother's exiled face.

35.

The village has its own sky,
        its own river,
its paths are unrepeatable
        among the tangle
        of bracken and fern.

It is visited by birds
        from the horizons of Africa,

26

who return annually
to build their own hammocks.

It has its own sun, its own moon,
 those unstable rings
 that remember it.
 Its cemetery is a treasury
of previous coffins and bones.
 On its gates stone lions
 snarl in silence,
 and its roses
 redden the air.
 Echoes everywhere,
 prints and resonances;
a single cloud
 is part of the narrative,
 of the story
 which bursts in fragrance
 from the dewless tips of bones.

36

The sun goes down
and is then reborn
 above paths, ruts:
under its rays
 the boys run
 towards their graves
 on bicycles:
 and girls too
 graduate to kitchens
 and the fierce breezes
of bedroom curtains.

All this has happened
 day after day,
 year after year,
 the sun a red
 ball that's returned
 every morning
 from over the wall.

From Italy
you come to our bare land,
from Venice
prodigious
with paintings.
Here the sky is clear,
lacks the fierce fire
of the Renaissance,
and the villages
sleep among sheep.

The drunks sing
Flower of Scotland to you
in echoing stations:
and the purple-crowned thistle
vibrates with thorns.
Tender Virgil,
dead in Mantua,
in the ice of perfection,
this is not your land,
you, exquisite saint
of the compassionate metre,
sleep elsewhere.
Our sun shines
(not burns)
beyond a grille of cloud,
and winter
is our typical season.
From Italy
you come to our sky.
It is like shifting
from a warm flat
to a lonely castle
hissing with ghosts.

38.

The rainbow arcs
at the end of the water:
it is a frail bridge
prepared by God.

In this field I find it,
then in another,
its fine colours anchor
among the sharp corn.

How strange it is
that angels can walk
among the cornfields,
the tares, the poppies,
the frail hint of blood.

The rainbow reminds us
that heaven is present
among the maggots,
the brown carriages of worms.

39.

Last night
I saw a snail
eating the cat's food.

Its mouth was busy
like a miniature snake,
its delicate horns
were tiny aerials
above the red plate.

Such a strange feeding,
this being from wet grasses
in the dry kitchen,

an alien entering
our warm kingdom,
with its black body
questioning our food.

In the garden
among the birds
my typewriter chatters,

It too has its own voice,
its astronomy of letters,
its interpretation of the world.

It too guards
its own territory
with ignorant metal.

Such happiness
among the green leaves
with its derived foliage.

41.

Cathy walks past,
and I am writing:
she sees through the window
my infirm hand.

"The corn is doing well,"
she told me this morning.
"After all, I'll take
the bread for my hens."

Such a marvellous light
that binds us together,
even I who grow
words on the page.

42.

Cat, today you caught a bird,
I found its feathers in the lobby,
and that, I must admit, disturbs me.

That the song should be stopped,
that the wings should be stripped,
from the slim body.

I don't mind you impaling mice
on the sharp protruding vice
of your claws.

But that you should have chewed the lark.
That you should have sent to the dark
the quick linnet.

I consider you, rising humpbacked,
a witch of the beautiful fact,
a thorny shadow.

And a white hunter, along the trench,
of the orange-breasted bullfinch
bitter-toothed one.

Who will nuzzle my shoulder
affectionately later,
bird-murderer,

feather-scatterer in the porch.
O let not in March
my songs be silenced

by that prowling inquisitive doom
which will devise harm
in a ring without mercy.

43.

You died
more a connoisseur of Latin
than of English.
> The rabbits played in front of your house
> but you did not notice them
> and as for the buzzard
> he was the unseen Caesar
> of your farm.

In togas they chatter among marble
      who were your obsession
      and the fountains of Rome
      jetted out of your garden.
      Virgil
      has written for your gravestone,
      and Ovid sings of exile
      in the depths of your library.
      It was a life of quotations
      that you lived,
      and an absence of mind
      your biography.
      It was only latterly
      that you really saw the sky,
      changeable:
      the wind of your century.
      As for the rest, footnotes,
      the relentless boredom of the classicist,
      the verb at the end of the sentence
      revealing at last your fate.

44.

The fire sparks up the chimney.
It is a hedge of thorns,
bright, purified, and simple.
Without it the art galleries
would have foundered in the marsh.

With it, the logs ignite
Rubens and Vermeer.
Statues replace glaciers,
and books, water.
Ghosts are born in fire.
They run about the world
breeding.

In summer
the blur of warm mist
    over the water,
    and the tall girls in green
    riding horses
along the level road,
clip-clop by shop-front.
Such mornings
    opening like books
fresh and novel,
    such fresh black shadows
humming among the leaves.

46.

The dog runs away
with the hen in his mouth.
Catch him!

He must not be allowed such traffic.
What bundle of feathers will be safe from him?
He will snatch the cockerel from the dawn.

Solid and meaty have been some of our poets,
our theologians, philosophers.
They can feel in their teeth
the theme of a new world.

Eat them thoroughly,
the bouquets of new stars.
Leave the bones, Copernicus,
to the starving Jesuits.

47.

The cat mews at the window
trying to get in.
It rears on its hind legs, like a stoat.

Beggar of the wind,
this is your house,
your fire is here.

It has the red sparks
of furious claws.

There were ghosts on my island
that chewed at the pane.
They were the many exiles
with their teeth of ice.

Why therefore should you not enter
with your eerie white fur,
having prospected all morning
for the absent mice?

48.

Art, how marvellous you are.
You bring us a birth,
a second birth in reflection,
and these reflections
seem more real than the real.

O wine red sky,
I burn in your vase.
O grave book,
I travel your winding road.

49.

Art,
     it is in the city
that you flourished,
were cherished
against the thirst of grass.
Redder than skies
     your reds,
and your greens
greener than mountains.

Your windows opened
on to a banded rainbow
that absolutely sang:
and nature does not know
your perfect circles.
     Breughel,
you brought your proverbs
     home in the evening;
Chagall, your bride and bridegroom
     waft through the air.

50.

Put out your paintings:
someone will notice them,
even in the passing,
in the wind of everyday.

Other poems

Nothing will Happen

Nothing will happen surely in this village
except adultery, sickness, harmless lies.

Listen, I watch the suns in their redness,
winding imperially around our stone,

and the absent-minded minister taking a walk
through these green clouds of his philosophy.

Nothing will happen surely... What's that?
Our crayon books are torn by strange shell fire.
A voice is shouting. There is nowhere safe.

And a dog digs for its bones under the holly.

The deer look down with their clear questioning eyes.

Not in Heaven

No, it is not in heaven that we find the dry
fine winds of fact,

but in the stones of March, Holy One,
in the knots of their essence.

Galilee, wind-dark sea, miracles,
there is no miracle greater

than the literature of April,
the manuscript of crocuses.

Shine, Holy One, from your narrow yellow niche
which has no clouds.

And let me have the ambiguous dapple of April,
the sigh of a forked breeze.

Helensburgh

I return to Helensburgh
where I used to see the green girls on horses
clip-clopping down the street.

Towards the Glasgow day trippers
with their breathless dogs and children
the tide rose slowly like silver.

At the fair,
the dodgems, painted with dragons,
turned in the salty air.

The retired pensioners
discussed their vague lives
through shrunken jaws and teeth.

In the spectacular evenings
the late sun touched
the Old Folks' Home with gold.

This is the town
of the mobile executives
to whom the Fair was a vulgar glare,

on a safe horizon
where nothing threatens
their gardens sheltered by walls.

And the old ladies with sticks
tottered up the brae
to the library to exchange romances.

And the Clyde lapped the shore
like an excitable dog
gray and masterless,

while the discontented young
toppled the benches
in the direction of the infinite sea.

The Drowned

It is true that the drowned return to us.
In the blue eyes of children we see them,
in a slight eccentricity of gait.

They spring actively out of the water, seeming
smaller than they were, bearing
large smiles, corn-coloured crowns.

Where the rocks are and the crabs manipulate
their bodies like toy tanks
in waters green and teeming like soup

they arise, clear-winged, articulating
sons and grandsons of themselves, stumpy
authentic chimes,

echoes, reflections, shadowy
waves that speak through the new waves,
underwritings, palimpsests,

a ghost literature behind another one,
carbons that have faint imprints on them,
blue veils of a fresh breeze.

Villagers

So many of those that I once knew
drowned in the Atlantic or the Pacific,
that unignorable and unknown blue.

Fishermen and part time footballers,
inadequate scholars, starers at dusty maps,
now forever locked in the sea's purse

with a miserly snap, while the guns tolled
over these restless acres, not to be ploughed,
at sunset fading into a foreign gold.

These guns which defended an empire
which wasn't, isn't, yours, who have drowned
ignorantly in sharp salt and fire,

who were once big figures in the twilight
where the river gently ran and chimneys bloomed
with a smoke sometimes grey and sometimes violet,

bone of my bone, my villagers, You have met
with the foreign-spoken stranger who has pulled
you inwards to his boat, his teeming net,

a random catch, I think not predestined,
gaping, slack-jawed, stubbly. Yet I sing
you breathless in the meshes long enchained.

Photograph of Emigrants

Your faces cheerful though impoverished,
you stand at the rail, tall-collared and flat-capped.
You are leaving Lewis (Stornoway) behind.
Before you the appalling woods will rise
after the sea's sharp salt, your axes hack
the towering trunks. What are you leaving now? –
The calm routine of winding chimney smoke,
the settled village with its small sparse fields,
the ceilidhs and the narratives. Deceived
by chiefs and lairds, by golden promises,
you set off, sailing towards a new world,
Canada with its Douglas firs and snow,
its miles of desolate emptiness.

Why do I weep
to see these faces, thin and obsolete,
these Sunday ties and collars, by the rail,
as the ship moves, and you move with it,
towards your flagrant destinies of sharp
bony starvation, ruinous alcohol.

All shall be revealed but at this time
your faces blaze with earnestness, and joy,
as if you were coming home instead of leaving.
Nothing will save some, standing by the rail,
others will come home in tartan caps,
a fury of possessions, and a love
of what's disappeared forever when they left,
themselves not being able to be there and here,
and therefore growing differently towards pictures
which frame them where they stand, thus staring out
into the inscrutable waters of their fates.

Incubator

The tiny baby sleeps in a cage of wires.
Lights blink on and off:

its legs are thin as matches, and its hair
a fuzz of limpid gold.

Sometimes it arches its tiny body,
stretches itself and yawns,

delicate as an egg in that machinery
which sings its own quiet tune.

Machine, you are my mother now, you feed
with the slow drop of time.

It is warm here, sleepless mother,
raise me to run one day

with my leather schoolbag among blossoms
on a day of lessons and fire.

Wakeful machinery, be good to me,
hear me if I don't breathe,

and ring your alarm bell, the panic
of your kind breast of steel.

Machine, let us sleep together,
on the bosom of the night,

till I grow tall, till I leave you
and seek soft human arms.

The Story

This is the story that I've always loved.
A little girl is running towards a bridge.
She leaves her tiny footprints in the snow,
and then suddenly becomes invisible.

Like the reader who leaves off reading the page,
Like the dying who have still some way to go.
There are first the footprints, then the unfathomable.
The Muse hasn't finished the good poem.

Perhaps it isn't good enough; perhaps
another poem takes over, yet another
better and more invisible song will come
out of the snow with a flaring of red banners.

Perhaps one day the ending will come back.
Now we aren't finished, but some day
after fresh experience we will find it,
having first tumbled from the bridge,

which is a rainbow from white heaven to here.
The little girl is ageing somewhere else.
She has run through a mirror to new country.
Drenched and flecked with snow, she has changed.

What is the future? Suddenly it breaks off.
This is a part of freedom, isn't it?
Years later she appears, no more a child,
but adult, unperplexed, her own mother.

Rainbow I love you, you are composed of light,
primary colours, hiatuses, a bridge.
Athlete and artist, you have perfectly curved
into the rich ignorance of the future.

At the Party

At the party everyone is talking.
Suddenly silence falls and you are alone
among the plates, the wine-glasses, the cups.
And there is no one to talk to but a limping man
who comes in late smoking a cigarette.
His face is gaunt and his frosty hair is wet.
And he coughs repeatedly and he says,
"This is my fifth party tonight.
I am rather tired and my appetite
is not as good as it used to be."

And there he is, graduate of frost and snow,
coughing repeatedly and saying No.

After the Edinburgh Festival

The Festival is over,
the Chinese acrobats have gone home
tumbling over piles of chairs across Europe,
dangling from the autumn skies.

Hamlet, wrapped in his black cloak, is brooding
among the colourful courts of the clouds,
hearing behind the curtains of leaves
a mortal song.

The Finnish poet has stopped reading
and is back among the pines
which stand like masts beside the lakes
in the country of the strange tongue.

The paintings hang in a gallery of the wind
showing harbours, people,
squares of an autumnal colour,
on which the night is falling.

The black troupe has returned to South Africa
and the sour smell of prisons,
their passes held humbly in their hands
in the debris of desolate camps.

Autumn remembers art
and the pipers who played at the castle
in a swish of sculpture
among the historical deaths.

Listen, is that the dry cold music of Stravinsky
bony, intellectual,
and the king in his suit of plague
bleeding volubly from the eyes.

Clowns, acrobats, actors,
you are our marvellous doubles
you keep the autumnal ice away
from the pools of evening.

You sing so high that the ice will break,
you put the dazzling crown from you,
your power is different,
yours is the glitter of cloaks,

the tinsel that illuminates the meagre,
the masks that face both ways,
the Januaries of ambiguity,
the consolation of defects.

And the acrobats on the edge of disaster
are saved by strong wrists,
and the lady who was sawn in half
jumps to her feet.

Resurrections, deaths, resurrections,
who is that black blind visitor
who sits patiently by the fire,
mortal ventriloquist,

whose tenement is falling apart,
while the stuttering landlord
is hopelessly free of his speech
in a room that is bordered with leaves?

Stupidly

Stupidly we stared down at our own hands
in the country of stupidity on a day
of autumn mist which wreathed about the trees.

We were the Bottoms with our asses' heads
among the miniature wrist-watches which ran
smoothly, impeccably, among the leaves.

We missed the small bright eyes that ruined us,
the purposeful, ambitious, colourful wings,
the fans of sunny morning in their zeal,

remembering only tales of a sweet justice,
the doors of mercy, wide poetic doors,
where tiny weasels pulsed at the throats of hares.

In this Pitiless Age

Somewhere in this pitiless age
I see the head of Dante leaning out of
the city of unemployed stars,

just, vigorous, condemning,
assigning to his three-line bars of flame
the loitering phantoms.

The thrifty system! Your justice killed the worst,
and not that Beatrice in a scent of rose
whom your soul rose towards so immortally.

Beyond it all the fragile climbing stairs
and that tremendous sentence luminous,
"The Love that moves the sun and the other stars."

Slowly

Slowly we are adopted by the words ... slowly we are other.
We are the aesthetic critics, not the ethical.
The play is a playful event.

Even agony becomes beautiful.
Even the broken heads are questionable.
Even the dictator's talent is in doubt.

No sounds from the street reach this theatre.
The torturer is a genius, or he is not.
The drapery on the coffin a lovely red.

The actor walks out on to a cold street.
Someone arrests him...someone tortures him.
His scream is no longer an actor's scream,

and yet the one from the theatre sounds like it.
The two screams meet where no one has a name.
They meet where all the walls have fallen down.

Meeting

I'm sure you don't know me, she said,
putting out her arms to me. On a wet day
in Lewis this was, among the dead.

Surely I know you, and she smiled.
You're Jessie, I said, and you stayed
in my village when I was a child.

So glad she was I remembered her, though dead,
her hair combed with salt, her hands
remembering the clothes' pegs she would fit

to the line once with her gallery of frocks.
Woolworths where we stood shone red.
I grew tired, she said, of the white clocks,

but you, you're different. And her mouth spread
like a seagull's in the wet and briny day.
I emigrated to the sea from dry land,

the waves attracted me with their energy.
But this is spring, isn't it, she said,
if you remember that clear cloudless sky

with no clothes in it. Yes, don't shed
tears, I answered. There is memory.
And took her fading hands. We are wed

to springs, autumns, visible and solid.
And watched her fade and fade past Woolworth's red
imitation jewels, like a seaward bird.

Marx

The ghostly superstructure reared up in front of you
from the time that the expropriated peasant
was turned into money.

From the time that the city became freedom's grave
and the usurer fattened on the farm
and the mortgaged fences.

All this grew more defined until one night
the structure of death reared up in front of you
disinheriting you:

the inevitable and determined one
who set out in the most beautiful urban evening
with a sickle in his hand.

The Women

See, the clouds are strolling along towards the sunset
in no hurry, almost unemployed,
except for the times when they are heavy with rain.
Sometimes they look down on the land
and admire the hills and the plain
before they are pregnant with rain.
Hand bags, wristwatches, sheer stockings, it was another country.
The milk makes us heavy. Now no lightning strikes
and there is the thunder of bottles on the stairs.
Give me my purse.
I shall set out
on a summer day. I'll spend the money I've not got.

In Belfast

The years' lessons are written on the walls –
No Surrender – Ulster Says No.
I see in the sky a Presbyterian rainbow,

orange and unforgiving, woven of fire.
To tear apart what oneself owns!
The nun strides through the city like a whore.

The present seethes about the Holy Book.
And drums tap on the coffins of the slain.
The tanks will ride tall through Genesis: masked men stalk.

O Rose of Sharon, modest and demure,
when among broken stones will you bloom once more
into an ordinarily guilty future,

Among the waste of broken iron, doors.
And men rather than angels greet across fences
the scoured tired eyes of pity and remorse.

Girl and Child

Trudging through the air of Homer for a sight of the bruised girl
    with the child
who stops at kiosks to wait for a telephone to ring
with his voice out of the clouds that have grown suddenly callous,
and a ring which she has not yet sold winking on her finger,
and the child's blue eyes staring out of its temporary nest,
I found only the scene where Andromache holds her child up to
    Hector
and with small fingers it touches the big shadowy helmet
before his death in a whirl of vulnerable dust.
And the battle is different and for the girl there is no Homer
and there is no memorial among the slums and lights of the city
as she stares into the windows at the bridal dresses and the furs
and slowly licks her lips as if she was tasting the last of her milk.

Speeding-up

Even the pace of the leaves seems to have accelerated,
even the children grow up more quickly:

even our dreeams turn into nightmares
and the statues are stalking away,

even the nights seem to have become one night
and the poems one poem:

and in all the airports of the world
the terrorists are reading the same books.

TV

This is your rectangle of narratives.
This is the voice that saves you from silence.

This is your scroll of perpetual images.
Listen, is there time for the poem to grow
in this incessant noise?

Is there time for that which is secret
to blossom?

Privacy must be paid for.

The blessed room, the refuge, the well, must be paid for.

When the comedians fade like ghosts grimacing in water
when the clowns remove their eyes,

the silence must be paid for, like water,
and the cell be precious

with silence, with fragrance, with the stone of privacy.

For the din is dreadful, the confusion of narratives is merciless,
the screen is vicious, it is a stadium of assassinations.

We need the bubbles of our own secret recesses,
the scent of clear water.

The narratives overwhelm us, they have no meaning, they have
    no connection with each other
We need the sacred light of the imagination.

We need the sacred cell and the pen that lies on the table.
We need the paper, that cool rectangle of white.

For one is heaven and sometimes the other is hell,
the world of frustrated murderers, the advertisements, the elegies
    without echo,
the questioners bending down to the bandaged ones,
the smiling humourless clowns.

The narratives overwhelm us, we need the white paper, unclouded,
we need in that furious hubbub a space for our names,
the sanity of prudent distance.

Christmas

This is the time when the egoes struggle for air,
when the television screen is a mishmash of narratives.
The children gather round the tree in simple greed,
and a horror film reproduces the agony of the Christ.
Love and goodwill are hard, there are so many contradictions
in the behaviour of those who are trying to be saints,
and then there are the others, bizarre in their avarice.
The too-often-sung carols lose their witchery,
even when the snow beautifully frames the windows,
and the hills are voluptuous with its whiteness.
Listen, what happened to that poor inexpensive manger
when so many are travelling towards it in newly-bought ski-suits
and furry collars which sparkle in the starlight.
This is the time for the family to assemble
and as on a treasure hunt dig up skeletons
and quarrel about hatreds which illumined their childhoods.
Where is there perfection? Even the child will be corrupted
by those who say, Why wasn't he given the proper family name?

The cameras burn holes in the fragilely human,
and lust and greed are perpetuated on the sideboard.
Who did not send us a Christmas Card this year?
We shall have our revenge on them. And who sent
a cheaper card than the dear one we sent them?
See how on the father patiently slicing the turkey
the son's eyes are fixed. Soon I will be your master.
I already feel the power refreshing my arm.

You neglected me often, he shouts to his exhausted mother,
I wasn't ever your darling, your jewel was really my sister.
Plain light but not love shines on the table.
Better to be alone with a cold compress on the head
lying on a bed and staring out at the stars
which are limitless, spendthrift, unused to pain or to ennui.
The riders of the past are coming with their treacherous parcels.
There are more than three of them and none of them wears a
    crown.
The whole white world is rented by the ambitious
and the noise of the television overwhelms literature.

Privacy may be metred like electricity or gas.
Dear night, someone is composing a carol
in Germany perhaps, in the heart of the Middle Ages,
far from the tables loaded with pheasant and wine,
and in the world of the mind, protected from all this racket –
the rotating narratives of films – the angels are flying
in the absolute country of the imagination, sustained
by the most terrible effort, trembling
in the middle of the night when no cries of the animals are to be
    heard.

The Country of Pain

In the country of pain there is the whimper of degradation,
and the man on the tall horse looks down on the defeated.

And the sir who has no imagination cannot suffer sorrow
since the land around him is a dazzle of mirrors.

He who sharpens his knife at the breakfast table and does not
    hear the cry
of the deprived and insulted dies the death of eternity,

and he who sings in the bathroom while the child drowns
will choke on the suffocating garbage of his own soul.

Listen, can you not hear it, the hum of Pain is everywhere
it whines over the tilled fields like the wires of telegraph poles,

and he who cannot see the dead for the flutter of silken flags
lies in a coffin of his own devising.

The soaked hats in the fields are like mushrooms,
and the careless whips return on the lightnings of time

to lie like snakes at the foot of the luxurious bed.
Stronger than poison is the venom of selfishness.

How shall the seasons forgive you and the songs of nightingales
and the glamour and splendour of roses, the humility of lilies –

how shall you correctly hear the notes of music
or scan with consonance the harmony of poems –

for all must be atoned for, the debts will some time be paid
and history will commemorate the coins that yourself have made.

Poor Artist

You who live on the dole and haunt the Oxfam shops,
how do you survive?

In the galleries there are paintings by Vermeer,
there are portraits of the opulent.

But how shall angel feathers spring from worn shoes,
and how shall the Madonna smile at you?

You have no room for a studio,
you must starve for your fresh paints.

And the landscapes look back at you without mercy,
and the still-lives have no serenity.

Let you paint the wine bottles of others,
the sweet apples on their plates,

Let you paint space without boundaries,
the sombre faces of the great.

How should art rise from the pavements,
sparse, moneyless, dizzy.

How should you not be troubled by the smile of the Mona Lisa,
by her expensive raiment?

The mystery is in the stones,
the mystery is in the ungovernable,

the desire for permanence.

So that clutching your paints you descend
to the Hades of the chaotic,

and in your mind a table without knives on it,
a table of perfect colour,

and on your feet the worn shoes you must paint,
the remedy of the actual.

Against Apartheid (I)

Those who beat the children
will die in the enchanted forest.

They will forever hear the whisper
of the leaves that will not fade.

Those who prepare the false mirrors
and the brews of poison

will turn into icicles,
in the caves of unknowing.

As they make rainbows from crayons
under the eyes of the stepmothers,

the children will be painting a history
that shows the tyrant as black,

obese, unhistorical shadows.
In the gardens of remembrance

the fountains will be sweet and merciful
only to the innocent and the wise.

Against Apartheid (II)

For you who have died in the silence of prisons, what prayers are
    enough?
For you who have been beaten to death,

who will never see the blossoms of your pain, the fruit of your
    broken bones,
the open and scented windows...

You are the alarm clocks that have been hammered by tyranny,
you are the complex wrist watches that rough hands cannot bear,
you are the imaginative ones.

I see you in the concentrated lights, blinking, exhausted,
I see you staring into the ardours of the future.

You have been accused of arching your bodies through windows
    like rainbows,
you have been accused of loving death.

Who loved life too much, its perfumes, its radiances,
who hated the cruelty of boots.

Who stared into eyes that have communed with stones
and for whom the human body is plasticine,

a pliable instrument from which all the music has been squeezed,
a careless melodeon.

You who have died in darkness may the future brighten,
for you who have died in silence may there be applause.

I say that your coffins will blossom with roses
when the earth will have devoured your enemies,

and that your bloodstained scripts will outlive their graffiti,
and that your triumph will be heard in the cells of violence,

and that your meagre calendar will be the beginnings of seasons
which will glow brilliantly in your broken spectacles.

Snow

Snow brings the soul to our land.
It brings the whiteness of eternity, it brings
a book with no print.

Snow, you are so lovely, you frame houses,
you lie in little white hills on the roofs,
you are the genial dictator of the night.

Slowly, gently, you transform the world
as from evil into good,
as from graffiti into origins.

The slums have disappeared, the rivers are silent,
the farms on the moors have become magical houses,
at which we call with white maps on our coats.

Only the spires out-soar the snow,
only the planes which travel sparkling,
only the sun which glows like a forge.

See, she plunges her hands into snow
who belongs to Africa,
whose poverty has not been hidden by it;
she drinks of its coolness.

And the children too enter this new country.
They build snowmen,
they put pipes in their mouths,
red buttons for noses.

Who does not love you, snow?
Magician of the night,
radical reformer,
instant utopianist.
Let us imagine you are eternal,
marvellous painter and sculptor,
let us sing your praises,
forgetting you are common water.

Cat and Mouse

The mouse's purple guts lie in a corner.
There was a battle of the innocent.
The cat threw giant shadows over the leaves.

To meet death with such immediacy!
In a smell of roses and of buttercups.
To feel the teeth deep inside your throat,

and, shocked by such a death, be paralysed
in a forest of tall grasses without music,
in a stadium of hot justice and of dew,

and a final meeting so unfortunate,
and somewhere the moon turning over and over
like a coin thrown carelessly by a distant hand.

The Leaves and Us

Running through the leaves we are not the leaves.
Living among roses we are not roses.
We are the forked indecisivenesses of history.

There are a million roads which we can take.
On each of them there are leaves and roses,
not the same roses but not so different,

as we are, the clever double ones,
in the scents which are pungent everywhere,
in the snow and ice which are everywhere the same.

Yet our summers are not theirs, nor our winters.
They do not see the role we give them
as part of our legends, of our history:

a certain leafy moon, a certain leafy night.
A story's made of transient foliage,
and forever afterwards we thirst for it.

In the Garden

I am bitten by the thorns of the roses.
They hang about my jacket in a fierce
clutch of claws, invisible and catlike.
My knuckles are a red astronomy
Such stars, such stars, such a new galaxy!
Prudence, my friend, does the rose mean so much,
and is perfection worth the sour thorns?
Somewhere I can hear a dog barking
at the invisible cat high in the rosetree.

Rose

Your exclusive shine, rose,
your colour that transcends relevance.

Blood of the inmost heart, triumph,
that which is transposed as it is:

in precise shape, fragrance. Nothing
is as exact as this:

the inmost torture astonished
into statement without history,

but itself, itself, itself,
rising from prison entire.

Autumn Stubble

The corn has been cut:
the stubble remains.
It is sharp and intense
in spite of the fences.
It will cut bare feet
not like the various
happy hilarious
seethe of the waving summer.
It has the crucial
bite of bright teeth,
this exciting satire.
Its rich dryness
invites us delightedly
as the swaying gossip of stalks.

The Cat

You were eighty-five when the cat appeared
one night at your door. It was perfectly white.
You wouldn't let it enter the house but you fed it
on scraps of fish which you placed on a blue plate.
It reared at your bedroom window like a stoat
mewing to get in: but you refused.
Sometimes you would threaten it with your fist.
What a strange white bony animal it was!
It would stare at you intently from the grass
and you would think: This thin beast troubles me.
My bones too are shaken as if he
were a sinister part of me, that had gone
hunting inquisitively about the stones.
The night before you died, it stared fiercely
in through the window, a tall vertical eel.
Its concentration was unshakeable.
And your bones melted and you lay at last,
a plate beside you, while your stubbly beard
had a fishy tang, wild, perilous, abhorred.

Early Spring

The primroses are out already
at the beginning of January.

And I have heard the birds sing.

Like Chaucer,
like the beginning of an idea,
like the hinge of a horizon.

Like happiness.
Like hearing the click of your heels
on the road outside my house.

And then as you climbed the stairs
your dress of yellow.

The Black Chest

When I opened the black chest there it was –
the pure diamond of the sweet alas
shining quietly like a teardrop.

In the distance I could hear
the fall of great houses, and the fire
of wills clashing in a new idea.

And also I could hear the scurry
of mice around the big tree
whence the cat glared down with green eyes.

Nevertheless there was a fragrance
from the black box: and a consonance
breathing from the lucky perfume,

though the gaunt face of the actor glowered
and among the waste moors shook the white beard
of the mad king, unfriended and defunct,

and though from the black box she rose
with white wings, throwing away her purse
of contradictions, and her candid verse.

The Traveller

The gates are open for you, stranger,
come in with your packet of narratives.

The wind has refined you
on your long journey.

What have you not seen? My imagination
cannot invent your stories.

For there is nothing more imaginative than life,
or more fortuitous.

And its epics have more fluctuations
than there are in Homer.

It was in another country entirely
that you recognised your fellow villager,

it was in a bar in Auckland
that you met your brother.

It was under the stars of Australia
that your mother drifted towards you

in a nightgown of dew,
in a bridal web of remembrance.

Life has mysterious corners
that the imagination doesnt know of,

and someone will enter at the denouement,
who wasn't in the dramatis personae,

and so it is that you may unpack your stories,
stranger, messenger of the wind,

and remove from it clouds,
waterfalls with well known portraits,

while the imagination will sit in a corner
listening like a pupil

to your stories of transformations,
the authentic detail of life.

Farewell my Brother

"Farewell my brother."
The seas separate us,
a history of salt.

It is as if I had dreamed
that on an island ringed by waves
we once walked

when the buttercups blew in the wind
around the ruins of houses
in a blank sea-gaze.

The Bible was a hard wall
which we climbed over
to touch the consolations of the heart.

Eternal voyaging!
Among the civil wars of Africa
you spent the best of your days.

You will lie in a different earth
far from Lewis
unlearned in your history,
with its own legends.

In the early morning
I heard a raven
squawking above my ground,
a rancorous wanderer
in his bad-tempered province.

Forgive us our misunderstandings.
Life is not like strolling,
carelessly through a field.

It is not sunset
over a stubble
colouring the sharpness,
a perfection of swords.

The earth shakes
often when we are surest
of the prosperity of our fortune.

Even when the moon
is round as a coin,
our achieved gamble.

Even as I wrote
you were absently sleeping
like an alien on this earth.

My distant brother,
with your own casket
of joys and tribulations.

Barer than the mind
is the soil of Lewis.
It is in the keeping of the wind.
It has the sea's resonance,

that constant music
that enchanted cottage
which enhanced our residence,

our hunger for the unknown.
If we could speak again
would we know better?

I offer this bouquet
from the oceans of salt,
my distant brother.

I send it across the seas
to the spaciousness of Canada,
my flowering poem,

to let its fragrance
be sweet in your nostrils,
though you are now unable
to converse with me.

My distant brother,
in the shelter of my poem
let you be secret

till we are children again
in the one bed
in the changing weather
of an inquisitive childhood.

The roads separate:
see, I wave to you,
you turn away completely
into your own cloud.

See, I wave to you
you are disappearing forever.
Tears disarm me.

Now you stand like a statue
in the honour of goodness.

My pride and my tears burn me.

Farewell, my brother.

Listen

Listen, I have flown through darkness towards joy,
I have put the mossy stones away from me,
and the thorns, the thistles, the brambles.
I have swum upward like a fish

through the black wet earth, the ancient roots
which insanely fight with each other
in a grave which creates a treasure house
of light upward-springing leaves.

Such joy, such joy! Such airy drama
the clouds compose in the heavens,
such interchange of comedies,
disguises, rhymes, denouements.

I had not believed that the stony heads
would change to actors and actresses,
and that the grooved armour of statues
would rise and walk away

into a resurrection of villages,
townspeople, citizens, dead exiles,
who sing with the salt in their mouths,
winged nightingales of brine.